SLOW COOKER DOG FOOD COOKBOOK FOR DACHSHUNDS

Dr. Wesley Glasgow

DISCLAIMER

TABLE OF CONTENTS

INTRODUCTION

In the heart of every dog lover lies a profound desire to provide the best possible care for their furry companions. For me, this journey began at a tender age when my parents gifted me my first dog, Dan. As a wide-eyed child, I was immediately enamored with Dan's playful antics and unwavering loyalty. He became my constant companion, my confidant, and my closest friend.

Like any doting pet owner, I wanted to spoil Dan with love and affection. And what better way to express my devotion than by indulging him with treats and lavish meals? I believed that showering Dan with food was an expression of love, a way to show him just how much he meant to me.

However, my well-intentioned gestures soon took a devastating turn. After a few blissful years together, Dan's health began to decline rapidly. He became lethargic, overweight, and plagued by a host of health issues. Alarmed by his condition, my parents rushed him to the veterinarian, where we received the heartbreaking news: Dan had been diagnosed with diabetes.

The weight of guilt and regret settled heavily upon my young shoulders as I realized the role my ignorance had played in Dan's suffering. I had unknowingly contributed to his poor health by feeding him a diet devoid of proper nutrition. It was a harsh lesson, but one that would shape the course of my life forever.

Determined to right my wrongs and ensure that no other dog would suffer the same fate as Dan, I embarked on a mission to learn everything I could about canine nutrition. I devoured books, attended seminars, and sought guidance from experts in the field. Armed with knowledge and a newfound sense of purpose, I dedicated myself to providing dogs with the nourishment they need to thrive.

Fast forward twenty-five years, and I stand before you as Dr. Wesley Glasgow, a veterinarian and passionate advocate for canine health and wellness. My journey from a young dog lover to a seasoned professional has been filled with highs and lows, victories and setbacks. But through it all, one thing has remained constant: my unwavering commitment to improving the lives of dogs everywhere.

Today, I am proud to introduce my latest endeavor: a slow cooker cookbook tailored specifically to Dachshunds. Having witnessed firsthand the transformative power of good nutrition, I am excited to share my expertise and culinary creations with fellow dog lovers around the world. But before we delve into the recipes that lie within these pages, allow me to share a heartwarming story that epitomizes the profound impact of this cookbook.

Not long ago, a devoted Dachshund owner approached me with concerns about her dog's weight and overall well-being. Her beloved pet, Max, had been struggling with obesity and related health issues for years, despite her best efforts to manage his diet. Desperate for a solution, she eagerly adopted my cookbook and began preparing the meals contained within.

What happened next was nothing short of miraculous. In just a few short weeks, Max underwent a remarkable transformation. He shed excess pounds, his energy levels soared, and his coat gleamed with newfound vitality. But perhaps most importantly, Max's zest for life returned in full force, as he bounded around the house with the boundless enthusiasm of a puppy.

The joy and gratitude expressed by Max's owner touched me deeply, serving as a poignant reminder of why I do what I do. It is stories like these that fuel my passion and reaffirm my belief in the power of good nutrition to change lives – both canine and human alike.

As we embark on this culinary journey together, I invite you to join me in unleashing the full potential of your Dachshund's health and happiness. Within these pages, you will find a treasure trove of delicious recipes, expert advice, and practical tips to help you nourish your furry friend from the inside out. But more than that, you will discover a newfound sense of connection and companionship as you bond over shared meals and shared moments with your beloved Dachshund.

So, without further ado, let us dive into the world of slow cooker dog food and embark on a journey that promises to delight the senses, nourish the body, and warm the soul. Together, let us celebrate the extraordinary bond between humans and dogs and honor the unwavering loyalty and love they bring into our lives each and every day.

Contact the Author

Thank you for reading my book! I would love to hear from you, whether you have feedback, questions, or just want to share your thoughts. Your feedback means a lot to me and helps me improve as a writer.

Please don't hesitate to reach out to me through

glasgowesley@gmail.com

I look forward to connecting with my readers and appreciate your support in this literary journey. Your thoughts and comments are valuable to me.

Chapter 1
Understanding Your Dachshund's Nutritional Needs

Dachshunds, with their unique physique and predispositions, require special attention to their nutritional needs. Tailoring their diet to accommodate their breed-specific requirements is crucial for their overall health and well-being. Here's a comprehensive guide to understanding and addressing your Dachshund's nutritional needs.

Breed-specific dietary requirements:

1. **High-Quality Protein**: Dachshunds thrive on diets rich in high-quality protein sources such as lean meats (chicken, turkey, beef) or fish. Protein is essential for muscle development and overall health.

2. **Moderate Fat Content**: While Dachshunds are prone to weight gain, they still need healthy fats for energy. Opt for moderate-fat diets to support their activity levels without risking obesity.

3. **Controlled Caloric Intake**: Due to their small size and tendency towards obesity, it's crucial to manage their calorie intake. Feeding guidelines should be followed diligently to prevent overfeeding.

4. **Joint Support**: Dachshunds are susceptible to joint issues like intervertebral disc disease (IVDD) due to their long backs. Diets containing glucosamine and chondroitin can aid in joint health and mobility.

5. **Small Bites**: Their small mouths benefit from smaller kibble sizes or moistened food to aid digestion and prevent choking hazards.

Health considerations for Dachshunds:

1. **Obesity Management**: Dachshunds have a propensity for obesity, which can exacerbate spinal issues. Maintaining a healthy weight through balanced nutrition and regular exercise is crucial.

2. **Digestive Sensitivity**: Some Dachshunds may have sensitive stomachs, requiring easily digestible foods. Avoid ingredients that commonly trigger digestive upset, such as grains or artificial additives.

3. **Dental Health**: Dental issues are common in Dachshunds. Opting for dry kibble or incorporating dental chews can help promote dental health by reducing plaque and tartar buildup.

4. **Skin and Coat Health**: Dachshunds may experience skin allergies or dryness. Diets rich in omega-3 fatty acids from sources like fish oil can support healthy skin and a shiny coat.

5. **Regular Veterinary Check-ups**: Regular visits to the veterinarian are essential for monitoring your Dachshund's overall health, including weight management and potential dietary adjustments.

Benefits of homemade dog food:

1. **Quality Control**: Homemade dog food allows you to select high-quality ingredients and avoid fillers, additives, and preservatives commonly found in commercial diets.

2. **Customization**: Tailoring meals to your Dachshund's specific needs, such as allergies or sensitivities, is easier with homemade food.

3. **Freshness**: Homemade meals can be prepared using fresh ingredients, maximizing nutrient retention and flavor.

4. **Variety**: With homemade food, you have the flexibility to introduce a variety of proteins, vegetables, and grains to ensure a well-rounded diet.

5. **Bonding Experience**: Involving your Dachshund in meal preparation can strengthen your bond while ensuring their nutritional needs are met.

Chapter 2
Getting Started with Slow Cooking for Your Dachshund

Slow cooking offers a convenient and nutritious way to prepare homemade meals for your Dachshund. By utilizing wholesome ingredients and adhering to safety guidelines, you can ensure that your furry friend enjoys delicious and healthy meals. Here's a guide to getting started with slow cooking for your Dachshund:

Choosing the right Ingredients:

1. **High-Quality Protein**: Opt for lean meats such as chicken, turkey, beef, or fish as the primary protein source. These provide essential amino acids for muscle maintenance and overall health.

2. **Healthy Carbohydrates**: Include complex carbohydrates like brown rice, quinoa, or sweet potatoes to provide sustained energy and fiber for digestive health.

3. **Nutrient-Rich Vegetables**: Incorporate a variety of vegetables such as carrots, peas, spinach, and broccoli to add vitamins, minerals, and antioxidants to your Dachshund's diet.

4. **Fats**: Use healthy fats like olive oil or coconut oil in moderation to support your Dachshund's skin and coat health and provide essential fatty acids.

5. **Supplements**: Consider adding supplements like calcium, glucosamine, or fish oil to meet specific nutritional needs or address health concerns.

Essential kitchen tools and equipment:

1. **Slow Cooker**: Invest in a quality slow cooker or crockpot with adjustable temperature settings and a timer function for convenient cooking.

2. **Food Processor or Blender**: A food processor or blender is essential for chopping and pureeing ingredients to the appropriate consistency for your Dachshund.

3. **Measuring Cups and Spoons**: Accurate measuring tools ensure the proper balance of ingredients to maintain nutritional integrity and portion control.

4. **Cutting Board and Sharp Knife**: These tools are necessary for preparing fresh ingredients and portioning meats and vegetables.

5. **Storage Containers**: Use airtight containers or freezer-safe bags to portion and store cooked meals for future use, ensuring freshness and convenience.

Safety tips for slow cooking dog food:

1. **Avoid Toxic Ingredients:** Certain foods like onions, garlic, grapes, and chocolate are toxic to dogs and should never be included in their meals.

2. **Cook Thoroughly**: Ensure all ingredients are cooked thoroughly to kill any harmful bacteria and reduce the risk of foodborne illness.

3. **Bone Safety**: Remove bones from meat before cooking, as cooked bones can splinter and pose a choking hazard or cause internal injuries.

4. **Portion Control**: Be mindful of portion sizes to prevent overfeeding and obesity, especially considering Dachshunds' predisposition to weight gain.

Chapter 3
Breakfast and Brunch Ideas

Chicken and Sweet Potato Hash

- **Cooking Time:** 4 hours on low

- **Servings:** 4 servings

Ingredients:

- 2 boneless, skinless chicken breasts, diced

- 2 sweet potatoes, peeled and diced

- 1 cup frozen peas

- 1 cup carrots, diced

- 2 cups low-sodium chicken broth

- 1 tablespoon olive oil

Instructions:

1. In a slow cooker, combine diced chicken, sweet potatoes, peas, and carrots.

2. Pour chicken broth over the ingredients, ensuring they are fully submerged.

3. Drizzle olive oil over the mixture.

4. Cover and cook on low for 4 hours or until chicken is cooked through and vegetables are tender.

5. Once cooked, allow to cool before serving to your Dachshund.

Nutritional Information: Calories: 220, Protein: 18g, Fat: 5g, Carbohydrates: 25g, Fiber: 5g

Turkey and Pumpkin Breakfast Stew

- **Cooking Time:** 6 hours on low

- **Servings:** 6 servings

Ingredients:

- 1 lb ground turkey

- 1 cup canned pumpkin puree

- 1 cup brown rice, uncooked

- 2 cups low-sodium chicken broth

- 1 cup green beans, chopped

Instructions:

1. In a skillet, brown the ground turkey over medium heat until fully cooked. Drain excess fat.

2. Transfer the cooked turkey to the slow cooker.

3. Add pumpkin puree, uncooked brown rice, chicken broth, and chopped green beans to the slow cooker.

4. Stir to combine all ingredients.

5. Cover and cook on low for 6 hours or until rice is cooked through and stew is thickened.

6. Allow to cool before serving to your Dachshund.

Nutritional Information: Calories: 290, Protein: 20g, Fat: 7g, Carbohydrates: 35g, Fiber: 6g

Beef and Quinoa Breakfast Bowl

- **Cooking Time:** 5 hours on low

- **Servings:** 4 servings

Ingredients:

- 1 lb lean ground beef

- 1 cup quinoa, rinsed

- 2 cups low-sodium beef broth

- 1 cup frozen mixed vegetables (peas, carrots, corn)

- 1 tablespoon olive oil

Instructions:

1. In a skillet, brown the ground beef over medium heat until fully cooked. Drain excess fat.

2. Transfer the cooked beef to the slow cooker.

3. Add rinsed quinoa, beef broth, frozen mixed vegetables, and olive oil to the slow cooker.

4. Stir to combine all ingredients.

5. Cover and cook on low for 5 hours or until quinoa is cooked through and mixture is thickened.

6. Allow to cool before serving to your Dachshund.

Nutritional Information: Calories: 310, Protein: 25g, Fat: 10g, Carbohydrates: 30g, Fiber: 5g

Salmon and Rice Porridge

- **Cooking Time:** 3 hours on low

- **Servings:** 3 servings

Ingredients:

- 2 salmon fillets, skin removed and diced

- 1 cup white rice, rinsed

- 2 cups low-sodium fish or chicken broth

- 1 cup chopped zucchini

- 1/2 cup diced tomatoes

Instructions:

1. In a slow cooker, combine diced salmon, rinsed white rice, broth, chopped zucchini, and diced tomatoes.

2. Stir to mix well.

3. Cover and cook on low for 3 hours or until rice is cooked through and mixture is thickened.

4. Allow to cool before serving to your Dachshund.

Nutritional Information: Calories: 250, Protein: 20g, Fat: 6g, Carbohydrates: 25g, Fiber: 3g

Turkey and Spinach Egg Scramble

- **Cooking Time:** 2 hours on low

- **Servings:** 4 servings

Ingredients:

- 1 lb ground turkey

- 4 eggs

- 1 cup chopped spinach

- 1/2 cup diced bell peppers

- 1/4 cup grated cheese (optional)

Instructions:

1. In a skillet, brown the ground turkey over medium heat until fully cooked. Drain excess fat.

2. Transfer the cooked turkey to the slow cooker.

3. In a bowl, whisk together eggs. Pour the eggs over the turkey in the slow cooker.

4. Add chopped spinach and diced bell peppers to the slow cooker.

5. Stir gently to combine all ingredients.

6. Cover and cook on low for 2 hours or until eggs are set.

7. Sprinkle grated cheese on top if desired.

8. Allow to cool before serving to your Dachshund.

Nutritional Information: Calories: 280, Protein: 22g, Fat: 15g, Carbohydrates: 10g, Fiber: 2g

Beef and Barley Breakfast Stew

- **Cooking Time:** 5 hours on low

- **Servings:** 5 servings

Ingredients:

- 1 lb lean beef stew meat, cubed

- 1 cup pearl barley

- 2 cups low-sodium beef broth

- 1 cup chopped carrots

- 1 cup chopped celery

Instructions:

1. In a slow cooker, combine cubed beef stew meat, pearl barley, beef broth, chopped carrots, and chopped celery.

2. Stir to mix well.

3. Cover and cook on low for 5 hours or until beef is tender and barley is cooked through.

4. Allow to cool before serving to your Dachshund.

Nutritional Information: Calories: 310, Protein: 25g, Fat: 8g, Carbohydrates: 30g, Fiber: 6g

Chicken and Pumpkin Oatmeal

- **Cooking Time:** 4 hours on low

- **Servings:** 4 servings

Ingredients:

- 2 boneless, skinless chicken breasts, diced

- 1 cup rolled oats

- 2 cups low-sodium chicken broth

- 1 cup canned pumpkin puree

Instructions:

1. In a slow cooker, combine diced chicken, rolled oats, chicken broth, and pumpkin puree.

2. Stir to mix well.

3. Cover and cook on low for 4 hours or until chicken is cooked through and oats are tender.

4. Allow to cool before serving to your Dachshund.

Nutritional Information: Calories: 240, Protein: 20g, Fat: 4g, Carbohydrates: 30g, Fiber: 5g

Turkey and Vegetable Frittata

- **Cooking Time:** 3 hours on low

- **Servings:** 4 servings

Ingredients:

- 1 lb ground turkey

- 4 eggs

- 1 cup chopped broccoli

- 1/2 cup diced bell peppers

- 1/4 cup shredded carrots

- 1/4 cup grated cheese (optional)

Instructions:

1. In a skillet, brown the ground turkey over medium heat until fully cooked. Drain excess fat.

2. Transfer the cooked turkey to the slow cooker.

3. In a bowl, whisk together eggs. Pour the eggs over the turkey in the slow cooker.

4. Add chopped broccoli, diced bell peppers, and shredded carrots to the slow cooker.

5. Stir gently to combine all ingredients.

6. Cover and cook on low for 3 hours or until eggs are set.

7. Sprinkle grated cheese on top if desired.

8. Allow to cool before serving to your Dachshund.

Nutritional Information: Calories: 280, Protein: 22g, Fat: 15g, Carbohydrates: 10g, Fiber: 2g

Beef and Green Bean Casserole

- **Cooking Time:** 4 hours on low
- **Servings:** 4 servings

Ingredients:

- 1 lb lean beef stew meat, cubed
- 2 cups green beans, trimmed and cut into bite-sized pieces
- 1 cup diced potatoes
- 1 cup low-sodium beef broth
- 1 teaspoon dried thyme

Instructions:

1. In a slow cooker, combine cubed beef stew meat, green beans, diced potatoes, beef broth, and dried thyme.
2. Stir to mix well.
3. Cover and cook on low for 4 hours or until beef is tender and vegetables are cooked through.
4. Allow to cool before serving to your Dachshund.

Nutritional Information: Calories: 290, Protein: 24g, Fat: 8g, Carbohydrates: 25g, Fiber: 5g

Salmon and Vegetable Omelette

- **Cooking Time:** 3 hours on low

- **Servings:** 3 servings

Ingredients:

- 2 salmon fillets, skin removed and diced

- 4 eggs

- 1 cup chopped spinach

- 1/2 cup diced tomatoes

- 1/4 cup diced bell peppers

Instructions:

1. In a skillet, lightly sauté diced salmon until partially cooked. Remove from heat.

2. In a bowl, whisk together eggs. Add chopped spinach, diced tomatoes, and diced bell peppers to the eggs.

3. Transfer the partially cooked salmon and egg mixture to the slow cooker.

4. Stir gently to combine all ingredients.

5. Cover and cook on low for 3 hours or until eggs are set.

6. Allow to cool before serving to your Dachshund.

Nutritional Information: Calories: 250, Protein: 20g, Fat: 10g, Carbohydrates: 10g, Fiber: 3g

Chapter 4
Nourishing Soups and Stews

Chicken and Vegetable Soup

- **Cooking Time:** 4 hours on low

- **Servings:** 4 servings

Ingredients:

- 2 boneless, skinless chicken breasts

- 2 carrots, peeled and chopped

- 1 sweet potato, peeled and diced

- 1 cup green beans, trimmed and chopped

- 4 cups low-sodium chicken broth

- 2 cups water

Instructions:

1. Place chicken breasts, carrots, sweet potato, and green beans into the slow cooker.

2. Pour chicken broth and water over the ingredients.

3. Cover and cook on low for 4 hours or until chicken is cooked through and vegetables are tender.

4. Remove chicken breasts from the slow cooker and shred using two forks.

5. Return shredded chicken to the soup.

6. Allow to cool before serving to your Dachshund.

Nutritional Information: Calories: 180, Protein: 20g, Fat: 5g, Carbohydrates: 15g, Fiber: 3g

Turkey and Rice Congee

- **Cooking Time:** 3 hours on low

- **Servings:** 4 servings

Ingredients:

- 1 lb ground turkey

- 1 cup white rice, rinsed

- 4 cups low-sodium chicken broth

- 2 cups water

- 1 cup chopped spinach

Instructions:

1. In a skillet, brown ground turkey over medium heat until fully cooked. Drain excess fat.

2. Transfer cooked turkey to the slow cooker.

3. Add rinsed white rice, chicken broth, water, and chopped spinach to the slow cooker.

4. Stir to combine all ingredients.

5. Cover and cook on low for 3 hours or until rice is cooked through and mixture is thickened.

6. Allow to cool before serving to your Dachshund.

Nutritional Information: Calories: 250, Protein: 20g, Fat: 7g, Carbohydrates: 25g, Fiber: 3g

Beef and Barley Stew

- **Cooking Time:** 5 hours on low

- **Servings:** 5 servings

Ingredients:

- 1 lb lean beef stew meat, cubed

- 1 cup pearl barley

- 2 cups low-sodium beef broth

- 2 cups water

- 1 cup chopped carrots

- 1 cup chopped celery

Instructions:

1. Place beef stew meat, pearl barley, beef broth, water, carrots, and celery into the slow cooker.

2. Stir to mix well.

3. Cover and cook on low for 5 hours or until beef is tender and barley is cooked through.

4. Allow to cool before serving to your Dachshund.

Nutritional Information: Calories: 280, Protein: 25g, Fat: 8g, Carbohydrates: 30g, Fiber: 6g

Salmon and Potato Chowder

- **Cooking Time:** 4 hours on low

- **Servings:** 4 servings

Ingredients:

- 2 salmon fillets, skin removed and diced

- 2 potatoes, peeled and diced

- 1 cup chopped broccoli

- 1 cup chopped carrots

- 4 cups low-sodium fish or chicken broth

Instructions:

1. Place diced salmon, potatoes, broccoli, and carrots into the slow cooker.

2. Pour chicken broth over the ingredients.

3. Stir to mix well.

4. Cover and cook on low for 4 hours or until salmon is cooked through and vegetables are tender.

5. Allow to cool before serving to your Dachshund.

Nutritional Information: Calories: 220, Protein: 20g, Fat: 6g, Carbohydrates: 20g, Fiber: 4g

Chicken and Lentil Soup

- **Cooking Time:** 3 hours on low

- **Servings:** 4 servings

Ingredients:

- 2 boneless, skinless chicken breasts

- 1 cup dried lentils, rinsed

- 1 onion, chopped

- 2 carrots, peeled and chopped

- 4 cups low-sodium chicken broth

Instructions:

1. Place chicken breasts, dried lentils, chopped onion, and chopped carrots into the slow cooker.

2. Pour chicken broth over the ingredients.

3. Stir to mix well.

4. Cover and cook on low for 3 hours or until chicken is cooked through and lentils are tender.

5. Remove chicken breasts from the slow cooker and shred using two forks.

6. Return shredded chicken to the soup.

7. Allow to cool before serving to your Dachshund.

Nutritional Information: Calories: 240, Protein: 25g, Fat: 5g, Carbohydrates: 20g, Fiber: 6g

Turkey and Vegetable Stew

- **Cooking Time:** 4 hours on low

- **Servings:** 5 servings

Ingredients:

- 1 lb ground turkey

- 2 potatoes, peeled and diced

- 1 cup chopped green beans

- 1 cup chopped carrots

- 1 cup frozen peas

- 4 cups low-sodium chicken broth

Instructions:

1. In a skillet, brown ground turkey over medium heat until fully cooked. Drain excess fat.

2. Transfer cooked turkey to the slow cooker.

3. Add diced potatoes, chopped green beans, chopped carrots, frozen peas, and chicken broth to the slow cooker.

4. Stir to mix well.

5. Cover and cook on low for 4 hours or until vegetables are tender.

6. Allow to cool before serving to your Dachshund.

Nutritional Information: Calories: 280, Protein: 20g, Fat: 8g, Carbohydrates: 25g, Fiber: 5g

Beef and Vegetable Ragout

- **Cooking Time:** 5 hours on low

- **Servings:** 4 servings

Ingredients:

- 1 lb beef stew meat, cubed

- 2 potatoes, peeled and diced

- 1 cup chopped carrots

- 1 cup chopped celery

- 1 cup chopped tomatoes

- 4 cups low-sodium beef broth

Instructions:

1. Place beef stew meat, diced potatoes, chopped carrots, chopped celery, and chopped tomatoes into the slow cooker.

2. Pour beef broth over the ingredients.

3. Stir to mix well.

4. Cover and cook on low for 5 hours or until beef is tender and vegetables are cooked through.

5. Allow to cool before serving to your Dachshund.

Nutritional Information: Calories: 290, Protein: 25g, Fat: 10g, Carbohydrates: 25g, Fiber: 5g

Chicken and Rice Soup

- **Cooking Time:** 4 hours on low

- **Servings:** 4 servings

Ingredients:

- 2 boneless, skinless chicken breasts

- 1 cup white rice, rinsed

- 2 carrots, peeled and chopped

- 2 celery stalks, chopped

- 4 cups low-sodium chicken broth

Instructions:

1. Place chicken breasts, rinsed white rice, chopped carrots, and chopped celery into the slow cooker.

2. Pour chicken broth over the ingredients.

3. Stir to mix well.

4. Cover and cook on low for 4 hours or until chicken is cooked through and rice is tender.

5. Remove chicken breasts from the slow cooker and shred using two forks.

6. Return shredded chicken to the soup.

7. Allow to cool before serving to your Dachshund.

Nutritional Information: Calories: 240, Protein: 20g, Fat: 5g, Carbohydrates: 20g, Fiber: 3g

Turkey and Lentil Stew

- **Cooking Time:** 3 hours on low

- **Servings:** 4 servings

Ingredients:

- 1 lb ground turkey

- 1 cup dried lentils, rinsed

- 1 onion, chopped

- 2 cloves garlic, minced

- 4 cups low-sodium chicken broth

Instructions:

1. In a skillet, brown ground turkey over medium heat until fully cooked. Drain excess fat.

2. Transfer cooked turkey to the slow cooker.

3. Add rinsed lentils, chopped onion, minced garlic, and chicken broth to the slow cooker.

4. Stir to mix well.

5. Cover and cook on low for 3 hours or until lentils are tender.

6. Allow to cool before serving to your Dachshund.

Nutritional Information: Calories: 250, Protein: 20g, Fat: 7g, Carbohydrates: 25g, Fiber: 5g

Salmon and Vegetable Chowder

- **Cooking Time:** 4 hours on low

- **Servings:** 4 servings

Ingredients:

- 2 salmon fillets, skin removed and diced

- 2 potatoes, peeled and diced

- 1 cup chopped broccoli

- 1 cup chopped carrots

- 4 cups low-sodium fish or chicken broth

Instructions:

1. Place diced salmon, diced potatoes, chopped broccoli, and chopped carrots into the slow cooker.

2. Pour chicken broth over the ingredients.

3. Stir to mix well.

4. Cover and cook on low for 4 hours or until salmon is cooked through and vegetables are tender.

5. Allow to cool before serving to your Dachshund.

Nutritional Information: Calories: 220, Protein: 20g, Fat: 6g, Carbohydrates: 20g, Fiber: 4g

Chapter 5
Wholesome Main Courses

Turkey and Vegetable Casserole

- **Cooking Time:** 4 hours on low

- **Servings:** 4 servings

Ingredients:

- 1 lb ground turkey

- 2 sweet potatoes, peeled and diced

- 1 cup green beans, trimmed and chopped

- 1 cup carrots, peeled and chopped

- 2 cups low-sodium chicken broth

Instructions:

1. In a skillet, brown ground turkey over medium heat until fully cooked. Drain excess fat.

2. Transfer cooked turkey to the slow cooker.

3. Add diced sweet potatoes, chopped green beans, chopped carrots, and chicken broth to the slow cooker.

4. Stir to mix well.

5. Cover and cook on low for 4 hours or until vegetables are tender.

6. Allow to cool before serving to your Dachshund.

Nutritional Information: Calories: 250, Protein: 20g, Fat: 8g, Carbohydrates: 25g, Fiber: 5g

Beef and Rice Pilaf

- **Cooking Time:** 5 hours on low

- **Servings:** 4 servings

Ingredients:

- 1 lb lean beef stew meat, cubed

- 1 cup white rice, rinsed

- 2 cups low-sodium beef broth

- 1 onion, chopped

- 1 cup chopped bell peppers

Instructions:

1. Place beef stew meat, rinsed white rice, chopped onion, chopped bell peppers, and beef broth into the slow cooker.

2. Stir to mix well.

3. Cover and cook on low for 5 hours or until beef is tender and rice is cooked through.

4. Allow to cool before serving to your Dachshund.

Nutritional Information: Calories: 280, Protein: 25g, Fat: 8g, Carbohydrates: 30g, Fiber: 6g

Chicken and Quinoa Stir-Fry

- **Cooking Time:** 3 hours on low

- **Servings:** 4 servings

Ingredients:

- 2 boneless, skinless chicken breasts, diced

- 1 cup quinoa, rinsed

- 2 cups low-sodium chicken broth

- 1 cup chopped broccoli

- 1 cup sliced mushrooms

Instructions:

1. Place diced chicken breasts, rinsed quinoa, chicken broth, chopped broccoli, and sliced mushrooms into the slow cooker.

2. Stir to mix well.

3. Cover and cook on low for 3 hours or until chicken is cooked through and quinoa is tender.

4. Allow to cool before serving to your Dachshund.

Nutritional Information: Calories: 240, Protein: 20g, Fat: 5g, Carbohydrates: 25g, Fiber: 5g

Salmon and Potato Bake

- **Cooking Time:** 4 hours on low

- **Servings:** 4 servings

Ingredients:

- 2 salmon fillets, skin removed and diced

- 2 potatoes, peeled and thinly sliced

- 1 cup chopped spinach

- 1 cup diced tomatoes

- 2 cups low-sodium chicken or fish broth

Instructions:

1. Layer half of the sliced potatoes at the bottom of the slow cooker.

2. Top with diced salmon, chopped spinach, and diced tomatoes.

3. Arrange the remaining sliced potatoes on top.

4. Pour chicken or fish broth over the ingredients.

5. Cover and cook on low for 4 hours or until potatoes are tender and salmon is cooked through.

6. Allow to cool before serving to your Dachshund.

Nutritional Information: Calories: 220, Protein: 20g, Fat: 6g, Carbohydrates: 20g, Fiber: 4g

Beef and Vegetable Stew

- **Cooking Time:** 5 hours on low

- **Servings:** 4 servings

Ingredients:

- 1 lb beef stew meat, cubed

- 2 potatoes, peeled and diced

- 1 cup chopped carrots

- 1 cup chopped celery

- 1 cup chopped green beans

- 2 cups low-sodium beef broth

Instructions:

1. Place beef stew meat, diced potatoes, chopped carrots, chopped celery, and chopped green beans into the slow cooker.

2. Pour beef broth over the ingredients.

3. Stir to mix well.

4. Cover and cook on low for 5 hours or until beef is tender and vegetables are cooked through.

5. Allow to cool before serving to your Dachshund.

Nutritional Information: Calories: 290, Protein: 25g, Fat: 10g, Carbohydrates: 25g, Fiber: 5g

Turkey and Lentil Casserole

- **Cooking Time:** 4 hours on low
- **Servings:** 4 servings

Ingredients:

- 1 lb ground turkey
- 1 cup dried lentils, rinsed
- 1 onion, chopped
- 2 cloves garlic, minced
- 2 cups low-sodium chicken broth

Instructions:

1. In a skillet, brown ground turkey over medium heat until fully cooked. Drain excess fat.
2. Transfer cooked turkey to the slow cooker.
3. Add rinsed lentils, chopped onion, minced garlic, and chicken broth to the slow cooker.
4. Stir to mix well.
5. Cover and cook on low for 4 hours or until lentils are tender.
6. Allow to cool before serving to your Dachshund.

Nutritional Information: Calories: 250, Protein: 20g, Fat: 7g, Carbohydrates: 25g, Fiber: 5g

Chicken and Vegetable Curry

- **Cooking Time:** 3 hours on low

- **Servings:** 4 servings

Ingredients:

- 2 boneless, skinless chicken breasts, diced

- 1 cup diced potatoes

- 1 cup chopped carrots

- 1 cup chopped bell peppers

- 1 cup chopped cauliflower

- 1 can (14 oz) coconut milk

- 2 tablespoons curry powder

Instructions:

1. Place diced chicken breasts, diced potatoes, chopped carrots, chopped bell peppers, and chopped cauliflower into the slow cooker.

2. In a bowl, mix together coconut milk and curry powder until well combined.

3. Pour coconut milk mixture over the ingredients in the slow cooker.

4. Stir to mix well.

5. Cover and cook on low for 3 hours or until chicken is cooked through and vegetables are tender.

6. Allow to cool before serving to your Dachshund.

Nutritional Information: Calories: 280, Protein: 20g, Fat: 12g, Carbohydrates: 20g, Fiber: 4g

Turkey and Pumpkin Stew

- **Cooking Time:** 4 hours on low

- **Servings:** 4 servings

Ingredients:

- 1 lb ground turkey

- 1 cup canned pumpkin puree

- 2 potatoes, peeled and diced

- 1 cup chopped carrots

- 2 cups low-sodium chicken broth

Instructions:

1. In a skillet, brown ground turkey over medium heat until fully cooked. Drain excess fat.

2. Transfer cooked turkey to the slow cooker.

3. Add canned pumpkin puree, diced potatoes, chopped carrots, and chicken broth to the slow cooker.

4. Stir to mix well.

5. Cover and cook on low for 4 hours or until vegetables are tender.

6. Allow to cool before serving to your Dachshund.

Nutritional Information: Calories: 270, Protein: 20g, Fat: 8g, Carbohydrates: 25g, Fiber: 5g

Salmon and Spinach Pasta

- **Cooking Time:** 3 hours on low

- **Servings:** 4 servings

Ingredients:

- 2 salmon fillets, skin removed and diced

- 2 cups cooked pasta (such as whole wheat or rice pasta)

- 2 cups chopped spinach

- 1 cup diced tomatoes

- 2 cups low-sodium chicken or fish broth

Instructions:

1. Place diced salmon, cooked pasta, chopped spinach, and diced tomatoes into the slow cooker.

2. Pour chicken or fish broth over the ingredients.

3. Stir to mix well.

4. Cover and cook on low for 3 hours or until salmon is cooked through.

5. Allow to cool before serving to your Dachshund.

Nutritional Information: Calories: 240, Protein: 20g, Fat: 6g, Carbohydrates: 25g, Fiber: 4g

Beef and Vegetable Chili

- **Cooking Time:** 5 hours on low

- **Servings:** 4 servings

Ingredients:

- 1 lb lean ground beef

- 1 can (14 oz) diced tomatoes

- 1 cup chopped bell peppers

- 1 cup chopped onions

- 1 cup chopped zucchini

- 1 can (14 oz) kidney beans, drained and rinsed

Instructions:

1. In a skillet, brown ground beef over medium heat until fully cooked. Drain excess fat.

2. Transfer cooked beef to the slow cooker.

3. Add diced tomatoes, chopped bell peppers, chopped onions, chopped zucchini, and kidney beans to the slow cooker.

4. Stir to mix well.

5. Cover and cook on low for 5 hours.

6. Allow to cool before serving to your Dachshund.

Nutritional Information: Calories: 290, Protein: 25g, Fat: 10g, Carbohydrates: 25g, Fiber: 6g

Chapter 6
Delicious Treats and Snacks

Chicken and Sweet Potato Bites

- **Cooking Time:** 3 hours on low

- **Servings:** 8 servings

Ingredients:

- 2 boneless, skinless chicken breasts

- 2 sweet potatoes, peeled and diced

- 1 cup chopped carrots

- 2 cups low-sodium chicken broth

Instructions:

1. Place chicken breasts diced sweet potatoes, green peas, and chopped carrots into the slow cooker.

2. Pour chicken broth over the ingredients.

3. Stir to mix well.

4. Cover and cook on low for 3 hours or until chicken is cooked through and vegetables are tender.

5. Remove chicken breasts and shred using two forks.

6. Mash cooked sweet potatoes and vegetables together.

7. Mix in shredded chicken.

8. Allow to cool before serving to your Dachshund.

Nutritional Information: Calories: 180, Protein: 15g, Fat: 3g, Carbohydrates: 20g, Fiber: 5g

Turkey and Pumpkin Biscuits

- **Cooking Time:** 2 hours on low

- **Servings:** 12 servings

Ingredients:

- 1 lb ground turkey

- 1 cup canned pumpkin puree

- 2 cups whole wheat flour

- 1 egg

Instructions:

1. In a mixing bowl, combine ground turkey, pumpkin puree, whole wheat flour, and egg.

2. Knead the mixture until a dough forms.

3. Roll out the dough on a floured surface to about 1/4 inch thickness.

4. Use cookie cutters to cut out biscuit shapes.

5. Place biscuits on a greased baking sheet.

6. Bake in the preheated oven at 350°F (175°C) for 20-25 minutes.

7. Allow to cool before serving to your Dachshund.

Nutritional Information: Calories: 120, Protein: 8g, Fat: 2g, Carbohydrates: 15g, Fiber: 3g

Beef and Cheese Mini Muffins

- **Cooking Time:** 2 hours on low

- **Servings:** 12 servings

Ingredients:

- 1 lb lean ground beef

- 1 cup shredded cheese

- 1 cup oat flour (oats ground into flour)

- 1 egg

- 1/4 cup water

Instructions:

1. In a mixing bowl, combine ground beef, shredded cheese, oat flour, egg, and water.

2. Mix until well combined.

3. Spoon the mixture into greased mini muffin tins, filling each cup about two-thirds full.

4. Bake in the preheated oven at 350°F (175°C) for 15-20 minutes or until cooked through.

5. Allow to cool before serving to your Dachshund.

Nutritional Information: Calories: 150, Protein: 12g, Fat: 5g, Carbohydrates: 10g, Fiber: 2g

Chicken and Sweet Potato Bites

- **Cooking Time:** 3 hours on low

- **Servings:** 8 servings

Ingredients:

- 2 boneless, skinless chicken breasts
- 2 sweet potatoes, peeled and diced
- 1/2 cup rolled oats
- 2 eggs

Instructions:

1. In a pot, boil the chicken breasts until cooked through. Remove and allow to cool, then shred the chicken.

2. In a bowl, mash the cooked sweet potatoes.

3. In another bowl, beat the eggs.

4. Combine the shredded chicken, mashed sweet potatoes, rolled oats, and beaten eggs in a large mixing bowl.

5. Mix until well combined.

6. Roll the mixture into small balls and place them on a greased baking sheet.

7. Place the baking sheet in the freezer for 30 minutes to firm up the balls.

8. Transfer the firm balls to the slow cooker.

9. Cover and cook on low for 3 hours or until the bites are cooked through.

10. Allow to cool before serving to your Dachshund.

Nutritional Information: Calories: 120, Protein: 10g, Fat: 3g, Carbohydrates: 10g, Fiber: 2g

Peanut Butter and Banana Treats

- **Cooking Time:** 2 hours on low

- **Servings:** 12 servings

Ingredients:

- 2 ripe bananas, mashed

- 1/2 cup natural peanut butter

- 1 cup oat flour (or finely ground oats)

Instructions:

1. In a mixing bowl, combine mashed bananas and peanut butter until smooth.

2. Gradually add oat flour to the mixture, stirring until a dough forms.

3. Roll out the dough on a floured surface to about 1/4 inch thickness.

4. Use cookie cutters to cut out shapes or simply cut the dough into squares.

5. Place the treats on a parchment-lined baking sheet.

6. Transfer the baking sheet to the freezer for 30 minutes to firm up the treats.

7. Transfer the firm treats to the slow cooker.

8. Cover and cook on low for 2 hours.

9. Allow to cool before serving to your Dachshund.

Nutritional Information: Calories: 90, Protein: 3g, Fat: 5g, Carbohydrates: 10g, Fiber: 2g

Apple and Carrot Dog Cookies

- **Cooking Time:** 3 hours on low
- **Servings:** 10 servings

Ingredients:

- 1 cup grated apple
- 1 cup grated carrot
- 2 cups oat flour (or finely ground oats)
- 1 egg

Instructions:

1. Preheat the slow cooker on low.
2. In a mixing bowl, combine grated apple, grated carrot, oat flour, and egg.
3. Mix until a dough forms.
4. Roll out the dough on a floured surface to about 1/4 inch thickness.
5. Use cookie cutters to cut out shapes or simply cut the dough into squares.
6. Place the cookies on a parchment-lined baking sheet.
7. Transfer the baking sheet to the freezer for 30 minutes to firm up the cookies.
8. Transfer the firm cookies to the slow cooker.
9. Cover and cook on low for 3 hours.
10. Allow to cool before serving to your Dachshund.

Nutritional Information: Calories: 70, Protein: 2g, Fat: 2g, Carbohydrates: 10g, Fiber: 2g

Cheesy Pumpkin Dog Biscuits

- **Cooking Time:** 3 hours on low

- **Servings:** 12 servings

Ingredients:

- 1 cup canned pumpkin puree

- 2 cups oat flour (or finely ground oats)

- 1 cup shredded cheese (choose a variety safe for dogs)

- 1 egg

Instructions:

1. In a mixing bowl, combine pumpkin puree, oat flour, shredded cheese, and egg.

2. Mix until a dough forms.

3. Roll out the dough on a floured surface to about 1/4 inch thickness.

4. Use cookie cutters to cut out shapes or simply cut the dough into squares.

5. Place the biscuits on a parchment-lined baking sheet.

6. Transfer the baking sheet to the freezer for 30 minutes to firm up the biscuits.

7. Transfer the firm biscuits to the slow cooker.

8. Cover and cook on low for 3 hours.

9. Allow to cool before serving to your Dachshund.

Nutritional Information: Calories: 80, Protein: 3g, Fat: 4g, Carbohydrates: 8g, Fiber: 2g

Blueberry and Banana Dog Muffins

- **Cooking Time:** 2 hours on low

- **Servings:** 8 servings

Ingredients:

- 2 ripe bananas, mashed

- 1/2 cup blueberries

- 2 cups oat flour (or finely ground oats)

- 1/4 cup plain Greek yogurt

- 1 egg

Instructions:

1. In a mixing bowl, combine mashed bananas, blueberries, oat flour, Greek yogurt, and egg.

2. Mix until well combined.

3. Divide the batter into greased muffin tins, filling each about 3/4 full.

4. Place the muffin tins in the slow cooker.

5. Cover and cook on low for 2 hours or until the muffins are set.

6. Allow to cool before serving to your Dachshund.

Nutritional Information: Calories: 100, Protein: 4g, Fat: 3g, Carbohydrates: 15g, Fiber: 2g

Turkey and Cranberry Dog Jerky

- **Cooking Time:** 4 hours on low

- **Servings:** 10 servings

Ingredients:

- 1 lb turkey breast, thinly sliced

- 1/2 cup dried cranberries

Instructions:

1. Preheat the slow cooker on low.

2. Arrange the turkey slices in a single layer on the bottom of the slow cooker.

3. Sprinkle dried cranberries evenly over the turkey slices.

4. Cover and cook on low for 4 hours or until the turkey is fully dried and crispy.

5. Allow to cool before serving to your Dachshund.

Nutritional Information: Calories: 80, Protein: 15g, Fat: 1g, Carbohydrates: 5g, Fiber: 1g

Carrot and Peanut Butter Pupcakes

- **Cooking Time:** 3 hours on low

- **Servings:** 6 servings

Ingredients:

- 1 cup grated carrot

- 1/2 cup natural peanut butter

- 1 cup oat flour (or finely ground oats)

- 1 egg

Instructions:

1. In a mixing bowl, combine grated carrot, peanut butter, oat flour, and egg.

2. Mix until well combined.

3. Divide the batter into greased cupcake liners, filling each about 3/4 full.

4. Place the cupcake liners in the slow cooker.

5. Cover and cook on low for 3 hours or until the pupcakes are set.

6. Allow to cool before serving to your Dachshund.

Nutritional Information: Calories: 120, Protein: 5g, Fat: 6g, Carbohydrates: 10g, Fiber: 2g

CHAPTER 7

Special Dietary Considerations Dogs with Specific Needs

Grain-Free Chicken and Vegetable Stew for Sensitive Stomachs

- **Cooking Time:** 4 hours on low

- **Servings:** 4 servings

Ingredients:

- 2 boneless, skinless chicken breasts, diced
- 1 cup chopped carrots
- 1 cup chopped zucchini
- 4 cups low-sodium chicken broth

Instructions:

1. Place diced chicken breasts, diced potatoes, chopped carrots, and chopped zucchini into the slow cooker.

2. Pour chicken broth over the ingredients.

3. Stir to mix well.

4. Cover and cook on low for 4 hours or until chicken is cooked through and vegetables are tender.

5. Allow to cool before serving to your Dachshund.

Nutritional Information: Calories: 250, Protein: 20g, Fat: 5g, Carbohydrates: 25g, Fiber: 5g

Low-Fat Turkey and Rice Congee for Weight Management

- **Cooking Time:** 3 hours on low

- **Servings:** 4 servings

Ingredients:

- 1 lb ground turkey

- 1 cup white rice, rinsed

- 4 cups low-sodium chicken broth

- 2 cups water

- 1 cup chopped spinach

Instructions:

1. In a skillet, brown ground turkey over medium heat until fully cooked. Drain excess fat.

2. Transfer cooked turkey to the slow cooker.

3. Add rinsed white rice, chicken broth, water, and chopped spinach to the slow cooker.

4. Stir to combine all ingredients.

5. Cover and cook on low for 3 hours or until rice is cooked through and mixture is thickened.

6. Allow to cool before serving to your Dachshund.

Nutritional Information: Calories: 240, Protein: 20g, Fat: 5g, Carbohydrates: 25g, Fiber: 3g

Limited Ingredient Lamb and Sweet Potato Stew for Allergies

- **Cooking Time:** 5 hours on low

- **Servings:** 4 servings

Ingredients:

- 1 lb lamb stew meat, cubed

- 2 sweet potatoes, peeled and diced

- 1 cup chopped green beans

- 1 cup chopped carrots

- 4 cups low-sodium beef or lamb broth

Instructions:

1. Place lamb stew meat, diced sweet potatoes, chopped green beans, and chopped carrots into the slow cooker.

2. Pour beef or lamb broth over the ingredients.

3. Stir to mix well.

4. Cover and cook on low for 5 hours or until lamb is tender and vegetables are cooked through.

5. Allow to cool before serving to your Dachshund.

Nutritional Information: Calories: 280, Protein: 25g, Fat: 10g, Carbohydrates: 25g, Fiber: 5g

Digestive Health Turkey and Pumpkin Stew

- **Cooking Time:** 4 hours on low

- **Servings:** 4 servings

Ingredients:

- 1 lb ground turkey

- 1 cup canned pumpkin puree

- 1/2 cup cooked brown rice

- 1 cup chopped spinach

- 4 cups low-sodium chicken broth

Instructions:

1. In a skillet, brown ground turkey over medium heat until fully cooked. Drain excess fat.

2. Transfer cooked turkey to the slow cooker.

3. Add canned pumpkin puree, cooked brown rice, chopped spinach, and chicken broth to the slow cooker.

4. Stir to mix well.

5. Cover and cook on low for 4 hours or until flavors are melded and stew is heated through.

6. Allow to cool before serving to your Dachshund.

Nutritional Information: Calories: 240, Protein: 20g, Fat: 6g, Carbohydrates: 20g, Fiber: 5g

Joint Health Fish and Vegetable Medley

- **Cooking Time:** 3 hours on low

- **Servings:** 4 servings

Ingredients:

- 2 salmon fillets, skin removed and diced

- 1 cup chopped carrots

- 1 cup chopped green beans

- 1 cup chopped broccoli

- 4 cups low-sodium fish or chicken broth

Instructions:

1. Place diced salmon, chopped carrots, chopped green beans, and chopped broccoli into the slow cooker.

2. Pour fish or chicken broth over the ingredients.

3. Stir to mix well.

4. Cover and cook on low for 3 hours or until fish is cooked through and vegetables are tender.

5. Allow to cool before serving to your Dachshund.

Nutritional Information: Calories: 220, Protein: 20g, Fat: 6g, Carbohydrates: 20g, Fiber: 4g

Allergy-Friendly Venison and Potato Stew

- **Cooking Time:** 5 hours on low

- **Servings:** 4 servings

Ingredients:

- 1 lb venison stew meat, cubed

- 2 potatoes, peeled and diced

- 1 cup chopped carrots

- 1 cup chopped celery

- 4 cups low-sodium beef or venison broth

Instructions:

1. Place venison stew meat, diced potatoes, chopped carrots, and chopped celery into the slow cooker.

2. Pour beef or venison broth over the ingredients.

3. Stir to mix well.

4. Cover and cook on low for 5 hours or until venison is tender and vegetables are cooked through.

5. Allow to cool before serving to your Dachshund.

Nutritional Information: Calories: 280, Protein: 25g, Fat: 8g, Carbohydrates: 25g, Fiber: 5g

Senior Dog Chicken and Rice Stew

- **Cooking Time:** 4 hours on low

- **Servings:** 4 servings

Ingredients:

- 2 boneless, skinless chicken breasts, diced

- 1 cup white rice, rinsed

- 1 cup chopped carrots

- 1 cup chopped green beans

- 4 cups low-sodium chicken broth

Instructions:

1. Place diced chicken breasts, rinsed white rice, chopped carrots, and chopped green beans into the slow cooker.

2. Pour chicken broth over the ingredients.

3. Stir to mix well.

4. Cover and cook on low for 4 hours or until chicken is cooked through and rice is tender.

5. Allow to cool before serving to your senior Dachshund.

Nutritional Information: Calories: 240, Protein: 20g, Fat: 5g, Carbohydrates: 25g, Fiber: 3g

Weight Management Turkey and Vegetable Stew

- **Cooking Time:** 3 hours on low

- **Servings:** 4 servings

Ingredients:

- 1 lb ground turkey

- 2 cups chopped cauliflower

- 2 cups chopped broccoli

- 2 cups chopped carrots

- 4 cups low-sodium chicken broth

Instructions:

1. In a skillet, brown ground turkey over medium heat until fully cooked. Drain excess fat.

2. Transfer cooked turkey to the slow cooker.

3. Add chopped cauliflower, chopped broccoli, chopped carrots, and chicken broth to the slow cooker.

4. Stir to mix well.

5. Cover and cook on low for 3 hours or until vegetables are tender.

6. Allow to cool before serving to your Dachshund.

Nutritional Information: Calories: 220, Protein: 20g, Fat: 6g, Carbohydrates: 20g, Fiber: 5g

Vegetarian Lentil and Sweet Potato Stew

- **Cooking Time:** 4 hours on low

- **Servings:** 4 servings

Ingredients:

- 1 cup dried lentils, rinsed

- 2 sweet potatoes, peeled and diced

- 1 onion, chopped

- 2 cloves garlic, minced

- 4 cups vegetable broth

Instructions:

1. Place rinsed lentils, diced sweet potatoes, chopped onion, minced garlic, and vegetable broth into the slow cooker.

2. Stir to mix well.

3. Cover and cook on low for 4 hours or until lentils are tender and sweet potatoes are cooked through.

4. Allow to cool before serving to your Dachshund.

Nutritional Information: Calories: 240, Protein: 15g, Fat: 1g, Carbohydrates: 45g, Fiber: 15g

Digestive Support Pumpkin and Turkey Casserole

- **Cooking Time:** 4 hours on low

- **Servings:** 4 servings

Ingredients:

- 1 lb ground turkey

- 1 cup canned pumpkin puree

- 1/2 cup cooked quinoa

- 1 cup chopped spinach

- 4 cups low-sodium chicken broth

Instructions:

1. In a skillet, brown ground turkey over medium heat until fully cooked. Drain excess fat.

2. Transfer cooked turkey to the slow cooker.

3. Add canned pumpkin puree, cooked quinoa, chopped spinach, and chicken broth to the slow cooker.

4. Stir to mix well.

5. Cover and cook on low for 4 hours or until flavors are melded and casserole is heated through.

6. Allow to cool before serving to your Dachshund.

Nutritional Information: Calories: 250, Protein: 20g, Fat: 6g, Carbohydrates: 25g, Fiber: 5g

OTHER BOOKS BY THE AUTHOR

INSTANT POT DOG FOOD COOKBOOK

DOG FOOD COOKBOOK FOR PICKY EATERS

AIR FRYER DOG FOOD COOKBOOK

SLOW COOKER DOG FOOD COOKBOOK

DOG FOOD COOKBOOK FOR SENSITIVE STOMACH

SCAN THE QR CODE TO SEE MORE BOOKS BY AUTHOR

CONCLUSION

As we near the end of this enriching journey delving into the world of slow cooker dog food tailored specifically for Dachshunds, I am overwhelmed with gratitude for the opportunity to share my passion and expertise with you. From the roots of my childhood as an avid dog lover to my current role as a seasoned veterinarian and dedicated advocate for canine health, this expedition has been a profound odyssey of growth, learning, and devotion to our furry companions.

Reflecting on my journey thus far, I am reminded of the pivotal moment when Dan, my beloved childhood Dachshund, fell ill due to poor dietary choices. Witnessing his suffering served as a poignant wake-up call, propelling me into a lifelong quest to unravel the mysteries of optimal canine nutrition. Armed with determination and fueled by love, I immersed myself in the study of nutrition, seeking to understand the intricate balance of ingredients that would not only tantalize a dog's taste buds but also nourish their body and soul.

As the years passed and my knowledge expanded, I discovered the remarkable potential of the humble slow cooker as a tool for crafting wholesome and nutritious meals for our canine companions. Its gentle cooking method preserved the natural flavors and nutrients of the ingredients, resulting in meals that not only satisfied a dog's hunger but also supported their overall health and well-being. It was a revelation that inspired me to channel my culinary creativity into the creation of this cookbook, tailored specifically to meet the unique needs of Dachshunds.

Throughout these pages, I have poured my heart and soul into curating a diverse array of recipes, each meticulously crafted to provide your Dachshund with a delicious and balanced diet. From hearty stews to comforting casseroles, each dish is a testament to the power of good nutrition to transform the lives of our furry friends. But beyond the recipes themselves lies a deeper truth: the profound impact that our choices as pet owners can have on the health and happiness of our beloved companions.

As we come to the conclusion of this culinary adventure, I want to express my heartfelt gratitude to you, the reader, for joining me on this journey. Your willingness to explore new horizons and embrace the principles of optimal canine nutrition is a testament to your dedication to the well-being of your Dachshund. I am humbled and honored to have played a part in your journey, and I am excited to hear your feedback and honest reviews of this cookbook.

Your insights and suggestions are invaluable to me, as they help me refine and improve my recipes for the benefit of dogs everywhere. So please, don't hesitate to reach out and share your thoughts with me. Together, we can continue to make a positive impact on the lives of our furry friends and ensure that they receive the love, care, and nourishment they deserve.

In closing, may your Dachshund enjoy many happy and healthy meals ahead, and may our shared journey inspire others to embark on their own quest for optimal canine nutrition. Thank you for your support, and may our paths cross again in the pursuit of our shared passion for dogs and their well-being.

BONUS 1:
Mental Stimulation for Dachshunds

Dachshunds are intelligent and curious dogs that thrive on mental stimulation. Providing opportunities for mental exercise is essential for their overall well-being and can help prevent boredom, anxiety, and destructive behaviours. In this bonus chapter, we will explore various ways to keep your Dachshund mentally stimulated and engaged.

1. Interactive Toys: Interactive toys are an excellent way to challenge your Dachshund's mind while providing entertainment and enrichment. Look for toys that dispense treats or require problem-solving skills to access rewards. Puzzle toys, treat balls, and interactive feeders are all great options. Rotate toys regularly to keep your Dachshund engaged and prevent boredom.

2. Training Games: Dachshunds are intelligent and eager to please, making them excellent candidates for training games. Teach your Dachshund new tricks, such as "sit," "stay," or "fetch," and practice them regularly to keep their mind sharp. Consider enrolling in obedience classes or canine sports like agility or rally obedience to provide structured mental stimulation and build a stronger bond with your Dachshund.

3. Scent Work: Dachshunds have an excellent sense of smell and love using their noses to explore the world around them. Engage your Dachshund's natural instincts by incorporating scent work into their routine. Hide treats or toys around the house or yard and encourage your Dachshund to find

them using their sense of smell. You can also try introducing scent-based games like "find the hidden object" or enrolling in scent detection classes.

4. Brain Games: Challenge your Dachshund's problem-solving skills with brain games and puzzles designed specifically for dogs. Activities like hide-and-seek, shell games, or the "muffin tin game" (where treats are hidden under cups in a muffin tin) can provide mental stimulation and keep your Dachshund entertained for hours. Get creative and experiment with different games to find what your Dachshund enjoys most.

5. Daily Walks and Exploration: Regular walks provide not only physical exercise but also mental stimulation for Dachshunds. Allow your Dachshund to sniff and explore their surroundings during walks, as this engages their senses and provides mental enrichment. Consider varying your walking routes to introduce new sights, sounds, and smells, keeping your Dachshund's mind engaged and stimulated.

6. Mental Stimulation Prevents Boredom: Dachshunds are intelligent dogs that thrive on mental challenges. Without adequate mental stimulation, they can become bored and may exhibit undesirable behaviours such as excessive barking, digging, or chewing. Providing engaging activities helps keep their minds occupied and prevents boredom.

7. Mental Stimulation Reduces Anxiety: Like many dogs, Dachshunds can experience anxiety when they are not mentally stimulated or when they are left alone for extended periods. Mental exercises such as training games and interactive toys provide a healthy outlet for their energy and can help reduce anxiety levels.

8. Mental Stimulation Enhances Learning: Dachshunds are quick learners and enjoy the opportunity to learn new things. Engaging in mental exercises such as training games and brain teasers not only stimulates their minds but

also reinforces positive behaviors and strengthens the bond between you and your Dachshund.

9. Mental Stimulation Supports Cognitive Health: Just like humans, dogs benefit from regular mental exercise to maintain cognitive function and mental acuity as they age. Keeping your Dachshund mentally stimulated throughout their life can help prevent cognitive decline and promote overall brain health.

10. Mental Stimulation Fosters Problem-Solving Skills: Dachshunds have a natural instinct to problem-solve, and providing them with opportunities to use their problem-solving skills can be both rewarding and enriching. Activities such as puzzle toys and scent work challenge your Dachshund to think critically and find creative solutions to reach a goal.

By incorporating a variety of mental stimulation activities into your Dachshund's daily routine, you can help them lead a fulfilling and enriched life while also strengthening the bond between you and your beloved pet. Experiment with different activities to find what your Dachshund enjoys most and make mental stimulation a fun and rewarding part of their day.

REVIEW PAGE

Thank you for choosing to embark on this journey with me through the pages of **"SLOW COOKER DOG FOOD COOKBOOK FOR DACHSHUND"** Your decision to invest in my work means the world to me, and I am deeply grateful for your support.

As an author, there's nothing quite as rewarding as knowing that my words have resonated with someone like you. Now that you've experienced the story, I would greatly appreciate your feedback. Your honest review is not only invaluable in helping me grow as a writer but also serves as a source of motivation to continue creating.

Please consider leaving a honest review on my book by scanning the barcode below it will take you to my Author central page you can find the book and leave a review.

Your support and encouragement mean everything to me. Thank you for being a part of this journey.

BONUS 2

30 Day Meal Plan

Day	Breakfast	Lunch	Dinner	Snacks
1	Scrambled eggs	Chicken and rice	Slow-cooked beef stew	Carrot sticks
2	Oatmeal with mashed banana	Turkey and sweet potato	Lamb and vegetable stew	Apple slices
3	Cottage cheese with blueberries	Salmon and quinoa salad	Pork and pumpkin stew	Green beans
4	Yogurt with strawberries	Tuna and brown rice	Chicken and barley stew	Cucumber slices
5	Boiled chicken with carrots	Beef and lentil soup	Turkey and vegetable stew	Blueberries
6	Scrambled eggs with spinach	Lamb and couscous salad	Beef and potato stew	Celery sticks
7	Cottage cheese with raspberries	Chicken and pasta salad	Pork and sweet potato stew	Bell pepper slices
8	Oatmeal with diced apple	Turkey and quinoa	Lamb and rice stew	Watermelon cubes
9	Boiled egg with mashed sweet potato	Salmon and barley salad	Chicken and vegetable stew	Broccoli florets
10	Yogurt with diced strawberries	Tuna and rice	Beef and quinoa stew	Zucchini slices

11	Cottage cheese with diced mango	Chicken and lentil salad	Pork and barley stew	Cherry tomatoes
12	Scrambled eggs with bell pepper	Beef and pasta	Lamb and potato stew	Peach slices
13	Oatmeal with grated carrot	Turkey and couscous	Chicken and sweet potato stew	Spinach leaves
14	Boiled chicken with peas	Salmon and potato	Pork and rice stew	Cranberries
15	Cottage cheese with diced pineapple	Tuna and barley	Beef and vegetable stew	Strawberries
16	Yogurt with diced kiwi	Chicken and rice	Lamb and quinoa stew	Cauliflower florets
17	Scrambled eggs with tomato	Turkey and pasta	Pork and couscous stew	Green peas
18	Cottage cheese with diced peach	Beef and lentil salad	Chicken and barley stew	Raspberries
19	Oatmeal with mashed blueberries	Salmon and quinoa	Lamb and vegetable stew	Orange slices
20	Boiled egg with mashed pumpkin	Tuna and sweet potato	Pork and potato stew	Carrot sticks
21	Yogurt with diced strawberries	Chicken and couscous	Beef and rice stew	Apple slices

22	Cottage cheese with diced mango	Turkey and barley	Lamb and pasta stew	Cucumber slices
23	Scrambled eggs with spinach	Salmon and rice	Chicken and lentil stew	Bell pepper slices
24	Oatmeal with diced apple	Tuna and quinoa salad	Pork and vegetable stew	Blueberries
25	Boiled chicken with carrots	Beef and potato soup	Lamb and quinoa stew	Celery sticks
26	Cottage cheese with raspberries	Chicken and pasta	Turkey and barley stew	Watermelon cubes
27	Yogurt with diced strawberries	Salmon and lentil	Pork and rice stew	Broccoli florets
28	Scrambled eggs with bell pepper	Tuna and rice salad	Beef and couscous stew	Cherry tomatoes
29	Cottage cheese with diced mango	Chicken and barley	Lamb and vegetable stew	Peach slices
30	Oatmeal with grated carrot	Turkey and sweet potato	Pork and pasta stew	Spinach leaves

MEAL PLANNER JOURNAL

Meal Planner

Week of:

Monday

BREAKFAST

LUNCH

DINNER

SNACK

Tuesday

BREAKFAST

LUNCH

DINNER

SNACK

Wednesday

BREAKFAST

LUNCH

DINNER

SNACK

Thursday

BREAKFAST

LUNCH

DINNER

SNACK

Friday

BREAKFAST

LUNCH

DINNER

SNACK

Saturday

BREAKFAST

LUNCH

DINNER

SNACK

Sunday

BREAKFAST

LUNCH

DINNER

SNACK

NOTES:

Meal Planner

Week of:

Monday	**Tuesday**	**Wednesday**
BREAKFAST	BREAKFAST	BREAKFAST
LUNCH	LUNCH	LUNCH
DINNER	DINNER	DINNER
SNACK	SNACK	SNACK
Thursday	**Friday**	**Saturday**
BREAKFAST	BREAKFAST	BREAKFAST
LUNCH	LUNCH	LUNCH
DINNER	DINNER	DINNER
SNACK	SNACK	SNACK

Sunday	**NOTES:**
BREAKFAST	
LUNCH	
DINNER	
SNACK	

Meal Planner

Week of:

Monday	**Tuesday**	**Wednesday**
BREAKFAST	BREAKFAST	BREAKFAST
LUNCH	LUNCH	LUNCH
DINNER	DINNER	DINNER
SNACK	SNACK	SNACK
Thursday	**Friday**	**Saturday**
BREAKFAST	BREAKFAST	BREAKFAST
LUNCH	LUNCH	LUNCH
DINNER	DINNER	DINNER
SNACK	SNACK	SNACK

Sunday	**NOTES:**
BREAKFAST	
LUNCH	
DINNER	
SNACK	

Meal Planner

Week of:

Monday	Tuesday	Wednesday
BREAKFAST	BREAKFAST	BREAKFAST
LUNCH	LUNCH	LUNCH
DINNER	DINNER	DINNER
SNACK	SNACK	SNACK

Thursday	Friday	Saturday
BREAKFAST	BREAKFAST	BREAKFAST
LUNCH	LUNCH	LUNCH
DINNER	DINNER	DINNER
SNACK	SNACK	SNACK

Sunday	NOTES:
BREAKFAST	
LUNCH	
DINNER	
SNACK	

Meal Planner

Week of:

Monday	Tuesday	Wednesday
BREAKFAST	BREAKFAST	BREAKFAST
LUNCH	LUNCH	LUNCH
DINNER	DINNER	DINNER
SNACK	SNACK	SNACK

Thursday	Friday	Saturday
BREAKFAST	BREAKFAST	BREAKFAST
LUNCH	LUNCH	LUNCH
DINNER	DINNER	DINNER
SNACK	SNACK	SNACK

Sunday	NOTES:
BREAKFAST	
LUNCH	
DINNER	
SNACK	

Meal Planner

Week of:

Monday	**Tuesday**	**Wednesday**
BREAKFAST	BREAKFAST	BREAKFAST
LUNCH	LUNCH	LUNCH
DINNER	DINNER	DINNER
SNACK	SNACK	SNACK
Thursday	**Friday**	**Saturday**
BREAKFAST	BREAKFAST	BREAKFAST
LUNCH	LUNCH	LUNCH
DINNER	DINNER	DINNER
SNACK	SNACK	SNACK

Sunday	NOTES:
BREAKFAST	
LUNCH	
DINNER	
SNACK	

Meal Planner

Week of:

Monday	**Tuesday**	**Wednesday**
BREAKFAST	BREAKFAST	BREAKFAST
LUNCH	LUNCH	LUNCH
DINNER	DINNER	DINNER
SNACK	SNACK	SNACK
Thursday	**Friday**	**Saturday**
BREAKFAST	BREAKFAST	BREAKFAST
LUNCH	LUNCH	LUNCH
DINNER	DINNER	DINNER
SNACK	SNACK	SNACK

Sunday	NOTES:
BREAKFAST	
LUNCH	
DINNER	
SNACK	

Meal Planner

Week of:

Monday	Tuesday	Wednesday
BREAKFAST	BREAKFAST	BREAKFAST
LUNCH	LUNCH	LUNCH
DINNER	DINNER	DINNER
SNACK	SNACK	SNACK

Thursday	Friday	Saturday
BREAKFAST	BREAKFAST	BREAKFAST
LUNCH	LUNCH	LUNCH
DINNER	DINNER	DINNER
SNACK	SNACK	SNACK

Sunday	NOTES:
BREAKFAST	
LUNCH	
DINNER	
SNACK	

Meal Planner

Week of:

Monday
BREAKFAST
LUNCH
DINNER
SNACK

Tuesday
BREAKFAST
LUNCH
DINNER
SNACK

Wednesday
BREAKFAST
LUNCH
DINNER
SNACK

Thursday
BREAKFAST
LUNCH
DINNER
SNACK

Friday
BREAKFAST
LUNCH
DINNER
SNACK

Saturday
BREAKFAST
LUNCH
DINNER
SNACK

Sunday
BREAKFAST
LUNCH
DINNER
SNACK

NOTES:

Meal Planner

Week of:

Monday	Tuesday	Wednesday
BREAKFAST	BREAKFAST	BREAKFAST
LUNCH	LUNCH	LUNCH
DINNER	DINNER	DINNER
SNACK	SNACK	SNACK

Thursday	Friday	Saturday
BREAKFAST	BREAKFAST	BREAKFAST
LUNCH	LUNCH	LUNCH
DINNER	DINNER	DINNER
SNACK	SNACK	SNACK

Sunday	NOTES:
BREAKFAST	
LUNCH	
DINNER	
SNACK	

Meal Planner

Month of:

Sun	Mon	Tues	Wed	Thurs	Fri	Sat